DONKEY KONG COUNTRY

Rumble IN THE Jungle

by Michael Teitelbaum

Interior Illustrations by Leif Peng

Troll

You won't want to miss

DONKEY KONG COUNTRY

Available from Troll wherever you buy books.

Produced by Creative Media Applications, Inc.
Art direction by Fabia Wargin.

This book is dedicated to Amelia.

Special thanks to Roy Wandelmaier, Susan Simpson, and James Stepien.

One

The morning sun glimmered brightly over Donkey Kong Island. Standing under his tree house, Donkey Kong looked up through the branches and smiled. "It's a beautiful day for flying," he said to Diddy Kong, the young monkey standing next to him.

"I can't wait!" replied Diddy excitedly. "I've been looking forward to this for weeks."

Suddenly the quiet of the jungle morning was shattered by the sound of an airplane engine roaring overhead.

"There he is!" shouted Diddy, pointing straight up. "Look!"

Donkey Kong looked up and spotted the plane. The custom-built flying machine looked like an oversized barrel that had sprouted wings and a tail.

The plane looped, then dove right at the ground.

"Something's wrong!" cried Diddy. "He's going to crash!"

Donkey Kong and Diddy ran for cover as the plane continued to plunge toward the ground. At the last possible second, the flying barrel pulled out of its dive and coasted to a smooth landing, right in front of the two Kongs. The cockpit door flew open and out stepped the pilot, Funky Kong.

"Just surfing the wind currents, dudes," said Funky Kong. "Nothing to get uptight about. Stay mellow, stay cool."

Donkey Kong cleared his throat. "Uh, we knew that," he said. "Funky Kong, I'd like you to meet my little buddy, Diddy."

"Hey there, dude," said Funky. "Ready for your ride?"

Diddy hesitated for a second, thinking about the landing Funky had just made.

"It's okay, Diddy," said Donkey Kong. "I've flown with Funky a lot, and I'm still around to talk about it. In fact, Funky's business is taking folks

from place to place on Donkey Kong Island. He's got lots of experience in the air."

Diddy put aside his fears and headed for the barrel plane.

"Here you go, Donkey," said Funky, handing him a walkie-talkie. "You can use this to talk to us while we're zooming through the sky."

Just then a voice called out from behind them. "Hold on a vine-swinging minute!" It was Cranky Kong, Donkey Kong's granddad. "What in the name of monkey madness do you think you're doing?"

"Diddy's going on his first plane ride ever, Pops," explained Donkey Kong.

"I hate flying!" snapped back Cranky Kong. "Why, if apes were meant to fly, they'd have wings. Yes, sir, I like it right here on the ground. And if you had any sense, you'd stay put with your feet firmly planted on the jungle floor!"

"I'll be okay, Cranky," said Diddy. "Funky's a great pilot."

"The coolest of the cool, little dude," said Funky. "Hop in!"

As Cranky continued to complain about how much he hated flying, Diddy climbed into the barrel plane, followed by Funky. Diddy's heart pounded with excitement as Funky started up the engines. "Hang on," said the pilot. "We're out of here!"

With a powerful *whoosh* that practically knocked Cranky and Donkey Kong over, the barrel plane took off. It soared above the trees into the sky.

"Whooo!" shouted Diddy, looking down at the jungle beneath him.

Donkey Kong heard him on the walkie-talkie.

"How are you doing, little buddy?" asked Donkey Kong.

Diddy's voice came crackling through the walkie-talkie's speaker. "This is great! I can see the whole island from here. We — whoaa . . . "

Funky took Diddy on a wild ride through the sky, looping-the-loop, plunging down until they were just above the treetops, and then pulling out of the dive at the last minute and soaring straight up.

"This is so cool!" Diddy shouted as the world rushed past him in a blur.

"I told you it would be," said Donkey Kong from the speaker on the cockpit's dashboard.

"Hey, Donkey," said Diddy. "I can see the snow-covered mountains, the ocean, the Tree Top Town—even the old ruins!"

"Better to see some of those places from the air than to be in them, that's for sure," said Donkey Kong.

Off in the distance Diddy spotted what looked like a huge city. "What's that?" he asked, pointing to the buildings that made up the city's skyline.

"That used to be the biggest city on Donkey Kong Island," explained Funky. "It's called Big Ape City."

Once again Donkey Kong's voice came from the dashboard. "Lots of folks on the island used to live there. But over the years more and more of them moved out. They moved to the jungles, caves, treetops, mountains, all over. The city fell into ruins. It's been completely abandoned for years and years."

"Oh, yeah?" said Diddy. "Well, if no one lives there anymore, how come I see smoke and lights coming from the city?"

"You got me, little dude," replied Funky. He pulled out his binoculars and peered into the distance. "Diddy is right, Donkey Kong. It looks like something's happening down there. I see black smoke. Pretty weird."

"Let's go check it out," said Diddy, hoping for an adventure. "We could probably fly there in no time!"

"Put the brakes on, little dude," said Funky, shaking his head. "I don't go looking for trouble, and most of the time it doesn't come looking for me. If anything weird is going on in Big Ape City, I'm the *last* guy who's going to stick his good-looking neck out to see what it is. Now just stay cool and enjoy the rest of the flight."

Diddy Kong was a bit disappointed, but he still enjoyed the rest of his first plane ride. Funky zoomed down for one of his hair-raising landings, which left Diddy squeezing his eyes shut and screaming with joy at the top of his lungs.

Back on the ground Diddy leaped from the plane, did a cartwheel, and ran over to Donkey Kong. "That was the most fun I've ever had!" said Diddy.

"I knew you'd like flying," said Donkey Kong, smiling.

"Bah! Flying!" groaned Cranky. "A waste of time if you ask me. There's nowhere any self-respecting ape would want to go that he can't get to on his own two hairy feet!"

Diddy turned to Funky, who had just stepped from the barrel plane. "Thanks a lot, Funky. That was great!"

"Anytime, little dude!" replied Funky. "Any old time."

Just then a beeping came from the cockpit of the barrel plane. "They're playing my tune," said Funky. "Someone must need a flight." Funky checked in with the beeper in his plane.

"I've got to go pick up a passenger on the other side of the island," explained Funky. "So I'm out of here. Stay cool and catch a wave if you can, dudes!"

Funky hopped back into the barrel plane and took off. As the plane disappeared from view, Donkey Kong realized he still had Funky's walkie-talkie. "Oops," said Donkey Kong. "I forgot to give it back."

"Why don't you turn it on and tell him?" suggested Diddy.

Donkey Kong flipped on the walkie-talkie. "Hey, Funky, forget something?"

"I guess I did," replied Funky, hearing Donkey Kong's voice come out his cockpit dashboard. "I'll pick it up after I make this passenger run. Oh, by the way, tell Diddy that the route I have to take to get my passenger will bring me right over Big Ape City. I'll take a peek down for him as I fly over."

A short while later the walkie-talkie beeped. Funky's voice came through, only now it was very faint and interrupted by loud static. ". . . I'm over . . . Big . . . City . . . very weird . . . flying pigs . . ."

"Did he say flying pigs?" asked Diddy.

"That's what it sounded like to me," said

Donkey Kong. "But it's hard to hear him through all this static."

"... pigs ... swarming around the plane ..." came Funky's voice again.

Then the Kongs heard a terrible sound from the walkie-talkie's speaker. "It sounds like gunshots or explosions!" said Donkey Kong, growing alarmed.

"... been hit ... going down ... going to crash!"

Then the speaker went silent.

Two

"**F**unky!" cried Diddy. "Something terrible has happened to Funky. Someone shot down his plane over Big Ape City."

"But there's not supposed to be anyone in that city!" replied Donkey Kong.

"I told you I saw smoke and lights," said Diddy.

"We've got to go find Funky," said Donkey Kong. "That's all there is to it."

"*Go?*" whined Cranky. "What do you mean *go?* To Big Ape City? Just how in the jolly jungle do you think you're going to get there?"

"On my own two hairy feet, Pops," replied Donkey Kong. "Just like any self-respecting ape would do."

"Now, look here you whippersnapper," said Cranky. "Don't get wise with me. Why, when I was your age I once walked from the top of the snow-capped mountains to the—"

"It's okay, Pops," said Donkey Kong. "You don't have to come along. Diddy and I will go." Then turning to Diddy he asked, "You with me, little buddy?"

"Any time, anywhere, Donkey!" said Diddy.

"Just a vine-swinging minute!" shouted Cranky. "Do you really think I'm going to let you go off on another adventure alone?"

"Thanks, Pops," said Donkey Kong. "I knew I could count on you."

Donkey Kong loaded his backpack with a variety of miniature barrels. The barrels could do different things—some could even explode. "You never know when you're going to run across a Kremling or two."

Kremlings were evil, lizard-like creatures who had come to live on Donkey Kong Island. They stole bananas from the Kongs, and their factory had polluted the island's air and water. Donkey Kong, Diddy, and Cranky had blown up the factory, but the Kremling leader, King K. Rool, had escaped along with his henchmen. Kremlings still infested the island, and were a constant annoyance to the Kongs.

When all their supplies were packed, the three Kongs set off through the jungle.

Soon the Kongs reached Tree Top Town at the edge of the jungle. Tree Top Town was made up of wooden platforms and huts built high in the trees. It was once an active ape community. But when the Kremlings began their assault of Donkey Kong Island, they overran Tree Top Town and now lived there themselves.

"We'll have to move quickly and quietly under the platforms," whispered Donkey Kong.

"I was navigating these jungles when you were knee-high to a baby baboon," said Cranky. "I'll lead."

"No, Pops, wait!" said Donkey Kong.

But it was too late. Cranky charged forward and tripped over a low vine. Suddenly floodlights burst on, lighting up the whole area. A loud alarm blared a warning to the Kremlings above.

"The darned place is booby-trapped!" shouted Cranky as he got to his feet.

'"That vine you tripped over must have triggered the alarm!" said Donkey Kong.

Kremlings dropped down from the platforms, and the Kongs were quickly surrounded by the evil beasts. "Get them!" yelled one of the Kremlings, and they all charged at the Kongs.

Donkey Kong grabbed an overhead vine and sprang into action. He swung into three charging Kremlings, feet first, scattering them like bowling pins.

Diddy went into his cartwheel attack, springing off his hands and toppling two more Kremlings.

Even Cranky got into the act, slamming several Kremlings on their feet with his cane, sending them hobbling into the bushes.

Donkey Kong dropped down off his vine and found himself surrounded by five more Kremlings. "Here, guys," he said. "Let me give you a hand." Donkey Kong opened his palm and slammed the ground using all of his incredible strength. His hand-slap attack shook the jungle floor like an earthquake, and the Kremlings went

17

flying off in all directions. Donkey Kong looked around. There were no Kremlings left standing.

Suddenly the Kongs heard loud booms from above. "The Kremlings are firing their barrel cannons!" shouted Donkey Kong. "Run for cover!"

Dangerous barrels showered down all around the Kongs as they dashed under a dense rubber tree. "Those cannons are up too high to reach by throwing our barrels," said Diddy.

Donkey Kong reached up and pulled down a low branch of the rubber tree. "This should do the trick," he said, taking a TNT barrel from his pack. Donkey Kong pulled the branch back as far as it would go. He placed the TNT barrel on the end of the branch and let it go.

The branch whipped around, flinging the barrel up toward the platforms.

"Fire one!" yelled Diddy.

The TNT barrel sailed right into the mouth of a barrel cannon and exploded, destroying the cannon. Using the branch, Donkey Kong flung

barrel after barrel up at the platforms, until all the cannons had been destroyed.

"Way to go, thrilla-gorilla!" said Diddy, jumping up to give Donkey Kong a high five.

"Not bad for a youngster," added Cranky.

"Come on," said Donkey Kong. "Let's get out of here."

The Kongs moved past Tree Top Town and soon came to the edge of the jungle. As they proceeded, the terrain got more and more rocky. They soon found themselves at the base of the snow-capped mountains.

Cranky began to complain. "If you think I'm climbing over this blasted blizzard hill, you've got another thing com—"

Cranky stopped at the sound of a distant rumbling. "What in the name of monkey madness is that?" he whispered.

The Kongs looked up and saw tons of snow racing down the side of the mountain above them.

"Avalanche!" they all screamed together.

Three

"There's nowhere to run!" said Diddy in panic. "There's too much snow!"

"We're finished!" cried Cranky.

"Maybe not," said Donkey Kong. He had spotted a tiny gap between two boulders at the base of the mountain. "In there," he said, pointing. "Hurry."

The three Kongs squeezed through the small opening.

"It's pitch black in here," complained Cranky when they were all inside. "I can't see my big hairy hand in front of my face."

Before anyone could respond, a deafening crash blocked out all other sound. It went on and on, like the roar of the ocean. Wave after wave of snow pounded against the boulders that separated the Kongs from certain doom.

And then it was over. The silence was eerie.

"Everybody all right?" asked Donkey Kong.

"Oh, just fine," said Cranky. "We're trapped behind a million tons of snow in total darkness. Never been better."

Donkey Kong knew from his granddad's familiar complaining that he was not hurt.

"I'm okay, Donkey," said Diddy Kong.

"Thataboy," replied Donkey Kong. "Now let's see where we are." Donkey Kong pulled a homemade flare from his backpack. It was made from a coconut, with a rope wick stuck in the top. "This light won't last long, but it will show us what this place looks like."

Donkey Kong lit the flare. The light revealed dank walls dripping with water and a high ceiling overhead. In front of them stretched a wooden walkway with a metal railing, leading deeper into the mountain.

"This must be one of the entrances to the caves and tunnels that lead through the mountain!" exclaimed Donkey Kong. "We're not trapped after all. We just need to find the right passageway to lead us to Big Ape City. We may actually have found a shortcut!"

"Yeah, but what happens when the flare burns out?" asked Cranky Kong.

"The last time we were in these caves we made friends with Squawks the Parrot," explained Donkey Kong. "He always carries a high-powered flashlight. He led us through the caves and tunnels once before. Maybe he can help again."

Donkey Kong took a deep breath. Diddy and Cranky knew what was coming, so they put their fingers in their ears. Donkey Kong let out a tremendous yell, using all of his amazing lung power. His cry for help echoed throughout the twisting, turning tunnels inside the mountain. As the powerful sound finally faded out, so did the flare, leaving the apes in the dark once again.

Several tension-filled minutes passed. Then in the distance a light flickered. "Over here!" called Donkey Kong.

"Squaaawk!" came the reply as the light moved closer. Squawks the Parrot appeared, carrying his flashlight.

"Thanks for coming, Squawks," said Donkey Kong. "I'm glad you heard my call."

"Are you kidding, Donkey Kong?" asked Squawks. "I'm sure that cry was heard clear through to the other side of the mountain! Hi, Cranky, Diddy. What brings you back into the caves?"

The Kongs quickly explained their mission to find Funky. Squawks agreed to show them the quickest route through the mountain to bring them to Big Ape City. He led the way with his flashlight.

After a long underground journey, Squawks finally brought the apes to the cave exit closest to Big Ape City. After thanking Squawks, who returned to the caves, Donkey Kong, Diddy, and Cranky stepped outside. Before them rose the skyline of Big Ape City.

"I haven't been here since I was your age, Donkey," said Cranky Kong. "Even then it was decaying and dangerous. Still, it brings back memories. I remember battling a short plumber named Mario. And—"

"Pops," interrupted Donkey Kong. "I hate to interrupt, but we're here to find Funky, remember? We'd better get into the city."

"All right! All right!" grumbled Cranky.

The Kongs marched ahead and were soon in Big Ape City. They expected to find an empty, lifeless place. Instead, the city was bustling with activity. When Donkey Kong, Diddy, and Cranky saw this, they gasped at the sight.

"Kremlings!" whispered Donkey Kong, guiding the others behind a building so they would not be spotted. "The entire city is filled with Kremlings!"

Four

Big Ape City was once the center of culture, entertainment, and business on Donkey Kong Island. But the city was abandoned many years ago. Now the Kremlings, who lost their factory thanks to the Kongs' heroic efforts, had taken over the abandoned city.

Donkey Kong, Diddy, and Cranky stood on a dirty street in the city, next to a warehouse, watching Kremlings scurry everywhere.

"They're using the city as their new base of operations," said Donkey Kong. "But why are they here?"

A large Kremling cart, being pulled by a team of Kremlings, rumbled down the street and stopped at the warehouse's loading dock. The Kongs ducked into a doorway to remain out of view.

Klump, one of King K. Rool's henchmen, jumped out of the cart and began barking orders. "I need this cart loaded and back to the factory within the hour," shouted Klump. "King K. Rool wants the new factory completed by the end of the week, and we're way behind schedule. So move it!"

Kremlings ran out onto the loading dock and frantically began loading equipment into the cart.

Nearby, the Kongs were filled with dread by what they had just heard. "They're rebuilding their factory here in Big Ape City," whispered Donkey Kong.

"That must be why I saw smoke while I was up in Funky's plane," said Diddy.

"I think we need to get a better look at what we're dealing with here," said Donkey Kong. "Follow me."

Donkey Kong quickly tiptoed around the side of the warehouse, followed by Diddy and Cranky Kong.

"I *hate* these adventures," grumbled Cranky as he hurried to keep up.

Donkey Kong led them on a climb up a far wall and onto the warehouse roof. From that point, high above the street, a horrible sight greeted them.

A short distance away in the heart of the city, an enormous factory was being constructed. This factory was ten times the size of the one the Kongs had destroyed. Although it was not yet completed, the factory's smokestacks were already pouring huge amounts of pollution into the air.

"If they finish that thing, it will release enough pollution to poison the entire island!" said Donkey Kong.

"I say we go to that factory and blow it up, like we did to the other one!" said Diddy, pounding his fist into his palm.

"It may not be that easy this time," said Donkey Kong, pointing at the factory. "Look." The Kongs could see Kremling guards patrolling the entire outside of the factory. "It looks like they beefed up security, big time."

Below on the warehouse loading dock, two Kremlings struggled with a heavy piece of equipment.

"What is this thing, anyway?" one Kremling asked the other. "It weighs a ton."

"I don't know," replied the other Kremling. "But it sure looks nasty." The large metal box they carried was filled with wires, electrodes, and straps.

Klump overheard the two Kremlings. "That, for your information, is King K. Rool's truth machine. That monkey pilot we shot down has still not revealed the true nature of his mission. He *claims* he was on his way to pick up a passenger. But this device will make him tell the truth, once we set it up at the factory."

On the warehouse roof the Kongs froze in fear. "They've got Funky in the factory," said Diddy. "They think he's a spy!"

Donkey Kong scratched his head trying to come up with a plan. "They're going to use that horrible machine on him. Unless we can get him out of there!"

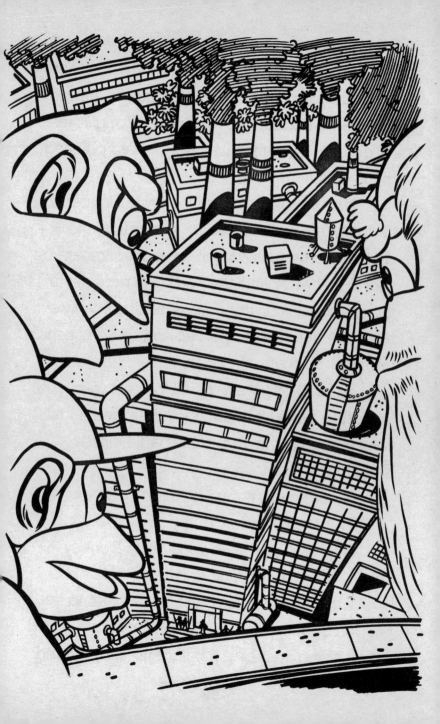

"And how in the name of monkey madness are you going to do that?" demanded Cranky.

A sly smile came over Donkey Kong's face. "We'll get him out in that cart," he said pointing to the loading dock below.

Cranky realized what Donkey Kong meant to do. "Why, back in my day we wouldn't be sneaking around, hiding in the back of carts," he snorted. "We'd battle the bad guys right out in the open. But you young apes wouldn't know a real adventure if it jumped up and bit you on the nose!"

Donkey Kong waited until the cart was loaded. When Klump and the other Kremlings went around to the front of the cart, Donkey Kong made his move.

"On three, we jump," he said.

"We *what?*" cried Cranky.

"Hop onto my back, Pops," said Donkey Kong. "Here we go. One, two, three!"

With Cranky on his back, Donkey Kong jumped from the roof. He was followed by Diddy. Using their best jungle skills, they landed as softly as they could on the back of the cart. They slipped under a canvas tarp that covered the equipment just as the cart rolled away, heading for the Kremlings' factory.

Under the tarp the Kongs could not have been more uncomfortable as the cart bounced along city streets filled with potholes.

"Something's sticking in my back," complained Cranky.

"I know, Pops," said Donkey Kong. "We're all uncomfortable. But if this works we'll get inside the factory and be able to find Funky."

The cart rolled on and soon came to the main entrance of the factory. The guard at the gate waved Klump through, and they entered the huge building.

The cart came to rest in a cargo room, and the Kongs heard Klump and his driver get off. "Call in the work crews and get this stuff unloaded now!" ordered Klump. The driver nodded, then ran off.

Klump walked around to the back of the cart. Beneath the tarp the Kongs could hear him breathing and snorting. Donkey Kong, Diddy, and Cranky sat holding their breaths, hoping they would not be discovered. Then Klump grunted and left the room.

"Next time you come up with a bright idea, leave it back in the jungle," said Cranky as the Kongs climbed from the cart.

"What now, Donkey?" said Diddy, stretching his legs.

"We've got to find a hiding place before the work crew shows up," explained Donkey Kong.

"Too late!" said Diddy as the doors to the cargo room swung open and 20 Kremlings ran toward the cart.

Five

"Down!" said Donkey Kong. "Under the cart. It's our only place to hide!"

Donkey Kong, Diddy, and Cranky crawled under the cart. They remained still as the Kremlings unloaded the equipment.

Soon all but two Kremlings had left.

"Where does this thing go?" asked one of the Kremlings, pointing at the truth machine.

"Klump wants us to take it to that ape pilot's cell," replied the other. The two Kremlings left the cargo room, carrying the horrible device.

The Kongs scrambled from beneath the cart. "If we follow those guys, they'll lead us right to Funky," said Donkey Kong. "Come on!"

Keeping a safe distance behind the two Kremlings, the Kongs followed them through the factory. Fortunately, the cell where Funky was being held was in a remote part of the factory, so the apes could easily stay out of sight.

When the Kremlings reached Funky's cell, the Kongs jumped into action.

Diddy jumped high in the air and landed on a Kremling's head, sending the evil creature to his knees.

"Hey!" shouted the other Kremling. "Where did you monkeys come from?"

"I'm not telling," said Donkey Kong. "But I can tell you where *you're* going. Right into that wall!" Donkey Kong curled up into his unstoppable barrel roll. He rolled into the second Kremling, sending him bouncing off the ceiling, then two walls, and finally to the floor, where he passed out.

Diddy came down for a second jump on his Kremling's head, and the big green creep joined his buddy in slumberland.

Funky ran to his cell door. "Man, am I glad to see you dudes," said the laid-back pilot. "How did you get into this uncoolest of places?"

Donkey Kong quickly told Funky Kong of

their journey. Cranky added the part about the uncomfortable ride in the Kremlings' cart.

"But enough talk for now," said Donkey Kong. "It's time for action!" He pulled a mini-TNT barrel from his pack. "Diddy, Pops, get back. Funky, move away from the door."

Donkey Kong tossed the barrel at the cell door. It exploded, tearing the locked door off its hinges.

"Thanks, big dude," said Funky as he joined the others and gave Donkey Kong a high five.

"If you two are through congratulating yourselves, I have a suggestion to make," said Cranky. "Let's run! That little firecracker you just set off is bound to attract some attention."

As the four apes ran back down the metal corridor, Funky filled in the others on what had happened to him. "First I was attacked by a squadron of flying pigs," began Funky.

"I *thought* that's what you said over the walkie-talkie," said Diddy.

"Those pigs must be the Krem-dudes' newest experiment," continued Funky Kong.

"Then cannonballs came out of nowhere and hit my plane. I crash-landed right next to the factory. As the Kremlings took me prisoner, I overheard that it was some kind of automatic defense system they've set up that shot me down.

"They had nothing against me personally. After all, who could? They just hate all Kongs, and so they threw me in that cage."

"Were you hurt, Funky?" asked Diddy.

"I'm fine," replied Funky. "But my barrel plane got pretty messed up. I think I can fix it, but I didn't have time to check out the damage. I heard them say that they hauled my plane to cargo room seven. I've got to get there and see what kind of repairs the old heap needs."

The Kongs rounded a corner and came face-to-face with a squadron of Kremlings, led by another of their leaders, Kritter. "I'm afraid you won't be seeing anything except the inside of your cell again!" snarled Kritter. "And this time you'll have company!"

Six

We're outnumbered, thought Donkey Kong. *Have to distract them.* He dropped down, opened his palm, and slapped the hard steel floor. The Kremlings lost their balance and toppled over one another. "Time for some masterful monkey maneuvers!" shouted Donkey Kong.

While the guards were still off balance, Donkey Kong jumped from Kremling head to Kremling head, knocking out the startled lizards. Diddy joined in, cartwheeling into three Kremlings at once.

Donkey Kong pulled a bunch of barrels from his pack and handed a few to Diddy and Funky. Although Funky Kong was usually too laid back to fight, he got into the spirit of things and hurled the barrels, smashing Kremling after Kremling.

Diddy climbed up the wall and hung from the ceiling, dropping barrels from above. "Bombs away!" he shouted as his barrels bashed more Kremlings.

The tide of battle had turned toward the Kongs, when suddenly Kritter and another Kremling grabbed Cranky. "Stop your assault or the old ape gets it!" shouted Kritter.

"Who are you calling an old ape, you big green toad?" yelled Cranky, as he elbowed Kritter in the stomach and bopped the other Kremling on the head with his cane. "Why, I was stomping on the likes of you when you were knee-high to a salamander!"

Donkey Kong smiled. "You've still got it, Pops," he said as he tucked into a barrel roll and took out the remaining Kremlings.

"Nice going, dudes," said Funky when the battle was over.

The Kongs raced through the factory, keeping out of sight. When they arrived at the cargo room holding Funky's barrel plane, they saw two Kremlings guarding the door.

Donkey Kong pulled two barrels from his backpack and handed one to Diddy. "I'll take the one on the left," said Donkey Kong.

"Ready when you are," said Diddy.

From their position down the hall, the Kongs tossed their barrels at the guards. The barrels struck, and the Kremlings fell to either side of the door.

"Time for a little brute strength," said Donkey Kong. He put his shoulder down, then charged into the door, bashing it off its hinges.

In the cargo room Funky Kong ran to his damaged plane. After a quick inspection he rejoined the others, who were standing guard at the broken door.

"There are a few things I can fix," said Funky, "but I'm going to need a new water pump."

"Where are we going to get that?" asked Donkey Kong.

"Right here in the factory," replied Funky. "Before they locked me up, the Kremlings dragged me all over the factory, from one leader to another, trying to figure out what to do

with me. I saw quite a bit of the place. I also saw where they keep their supplies."

"So let's go get a water pump," Donkey Kong said.

"The problem is," said Funky, "that even if I can fly us out of here, we'll be shot down by the automatic defense system again."

"I'll take care of that," said Donkey Kong. "Did you see where the defense system was?"

Funky nodded, then reached into his plane to pull out some paper and a pencil. He drew two maps. "One map shows where the supply room is. The other shows how to get to the defense system control room."

"We'll have to split up," said Donkey Kong, taking the maps from Funky and handing one to Diddy. "You up to it, Diddy?"

"You bet," said Diddy proudly.

Donkey Kong turned to Cranky. "Pops, I need you to stay here and help Funky in any way you can," he said.

"Fine with me," grumbled Cranky. "The last thing I want to do is run around this Kremling hotel."

"Good," said Donkey Kong, reaching into his pack and pulling out a few barrels. "Diddy, take some of these with you, just in case. Grab the water pump and meet back here. Good luck, little buddy. Let's get moving."

As Donkey Kong and Diddy left the cargo room, Funky pulled out his toolbox and got to work doing the repairs he could manage without the new parts.

Cranky Kong handed Funky the tools he needed and told story after story of his youth. Funky nodded a lot as he worked on the plane.

Donkey Kong headed toward the control room for the automatic defense system. *According to the map,* thought Donkey Kong, *it's eight flights up. I can't just stroll into the elevator or stairway without getting caught, so I've got to find another way to get up there.*

Just then Donkey Kong heard a group of Kremlings heading in his direction. He looked around. There appeared to be nowhere to hide. Then he spotted an air vent in the wall.

He pulled the metal grating off the vent,

climbed up into it, and pulled the grating back on from the inside. Unfortunately for Donkey Kong, the Kremlings who arrived were a work crew assigned to repair the vent he had just entered.

"I'll pull the grating off, you get out the tools," said one of the Kremlings.

Donkey Kong turned and crawled as fast he could, moving away from the grating, going deeper into the air shaft. He kept crawling until he came to a point where the shaft split left and right. The right side was labeled Air Shaft 162; the left side, Elevator Shaft 25.

I'm in luck, thought Donkey Kong. *If I can reach the elevator shaft, I can just climb right up the cables until I reach the floor I need. It will be just like climbing vines back in the jungle!*

Donkey Kong crawled along the shaft leading left until he came to another opening covered by a grating. Popping the grating off, he peered into the elevator shaft. Looking down, he saw the top of the elevator car several stories below. Looking up, he saw the shaft leading to the top story of the factory, some 20 floors above him. Straight ahead hung the steel cables that pulled the elevator.

Donkey Kong made the short leap from the air shaft to the cables and began the climb to the eighth floor. He was halfway to his destination when he heard a noise that sent a shock of fear through his body. It was a low, electric hum. He looked down and saw the top of the elevator car rushing up toward him!

Seven

Donkey Kong's heart was pounding furiously. He pulled himself up the metal cables, hand over hand, as fast as his arms would move. *It's catching up,* he thought, glancing down at the elevator. *Don't look down, just climb. Don't look down, just climb,* he repeated to himself over and over.

With the top of the car only inches from his feet, Donkey Kong reached the eighth floor. *Got to time this just right,* he thought. He kicked out with his powerful legs and smashed open the door to the eighth floor. The force of the kick carried his body through the door. The elevator car zipped by, just barely missing him.

Donkey Kong landed in a heap on the floor. He was breathing hard from the effort, but he had

made it. He was on the eighth floor, facing the door leading to the automatic defense system.

He stood up and was immediately grabbed from behind. "Next time just take the elevator like everyone else." It was Krusha, the biggest and strongest of all the Kremlings. "It's the end of the line for you, Kong," said the muscle-bound Kremling. "I'm taking you to King K. Rool."

Although Krusha may have been the strongest Kremling, fortunately for Donkey Kong he was not one of the brightest.

"Listen, Krusha, how'd you like to *really* impress Rool?" asked Donkey Kong.

"How could I do that?" asked Krusha, growing curious, though he still kept his tight bear hug around Donkey Kong.

"In my backpack, written on a piece of paper, are the locations of all the Kongs on Donkey Kong Island," said Donkey Kong. "Wouldn't you like to know where all the Kongs are so you can kidnap them and make your boss happy?"

"I sure would!" said Krusha excitedly.

"Then let go of my arms, and I'll get you the info," said Donkey Kong. Krusha loosened his hold. "You know where all the Kongs are?" asked Donkey Kong, reaching into his pack.

"Where?" asked Krusha.

"In the jungle! Where else?" cried Donkey Kong, who pulled a barrel out of his backpack and tossed it at Krusha.

The barrel caused Krusha to stumble, but that was all Donkey Kong needed. He barrel-rolled the brute off his feet, then double-jumped him until the Kremling was out cold.

Good thing these Kremlings are dumber than tree stumps, thought Donkey Kong as he kicked open the door to the defense-system control room. He tossed a TNT barrel into the room.

"You won't be shooting Funky down again any time soon," he said as the barrel exploded, destroying the system.

Donkey Kong reached the elevator shaft. *I don't like going back in here,* he thought, *but down has got to be easier than up.* He checked the floor indicator at the elevator door. The car was on the twentieth floor, at the very top of the factory. *I should make it down eight floors before the car comes my way,* he thought. Then he jumped back onto the cables and slid down to the air vent, crawling back inside.

Donkey Kong soon reached the other end of the vent. The work crews were gone, and so he slipped back out and hurried to the plane.

• • • • • •

During all this time Diddy was on a mission of his own. He had to get the water pump for Funky's engine. The supply room Diddy needed was located at the end of a series of catwalks extending upward, level after level.

The room I need is just off the fourth catwalk, he thought. *But if I just stroll right onto it, I'm sure to be caught.* Diddy stood at the beginning of the fourth catwalk and looked up. *What if I crawled along the* bottom *of the fifth catwalk, just above the one I need? As long as no one looks up from the fourth or down from the fifth, I'll be all right.*

Diddy leaped and caught hold of the bottom of the fifth crosswalk. The tiny holes in the metal plates were just big enough for his small fingers and toes to grip. He slowly made his way toward the supply room, pausing whenever a Kremling walked by below or above him.

When he reached the room, he waited until it was clear and then dropped down to the catwalk. Diddy tried the supply-room door. It opened easily. *This is lucky,* he thought. *Someone left it unlocked.* Diddy opened the door and slipped into the room.

There, doing an inventory of supplies, was Klap Trap, a four-legged Kremling with huge jaws and long, razor-sharp teeth. He growled at Diddy, who immediately jumped right at the Kremling.

But Klap Trap was quick. He stepped out of the way of the attack, just in time for Diddy to crash into a storage shelf. Boxes tumbled down on top of Diddy, who looked up to see Klap Trap charging at him, his massive jaws opened wide.

Diddy pulled out the barrel that Donkey Kong had given him. Klap Trap lunged right at Diddy, who stuck the barrel into the Kremling's mouth, then rolled out of the way.

Klap Trap snarled frantically. The barrel was lodged between his jaws, wedging them open. He couldn't close his mouth. As Klap Trap struggled with the barrel, Diddy grabbed a water pump and left, locking the door behind him.

Diddy's return trip along the bottom of the catwalk was uneventful, and the three Kongs were soon back at the barrel plane.

"Nice work, dudes," said Funky. "I'll have this baby back together in no time!"

As Funky repaired his engine, Donkey Kong, Diddy, and Cranky stood watch at the door. Soon the plane was ready to fly. "Funky Airlines, flight number one is leaving," announced Funky. "Right now! Hop in, dudes!"

"I hate flying," said Cranky as he climbed on board.

"Yippee!" shouted Diddy, following Cranky in. "Another plane ride!"

As Donkey Kong stepped into the plane, a squadron of Kremlings led by Rock Kroc arrived at the door. "So this is where you've been hiding! Attack!" he shouted.

Eight

Donkey Kong leaped into the cockpit next to Funky, who already had the engines racing. He pulled out a TNT barrel and flung it against the far wall of the room. The barrel exploded, ripping a big hole in the wall. "You're cleared for takeoff, Captain," said Donkey Kong as Funky engaged the throttle and the plane rolled forward.

Rock Kroc and the others reached the plane just as it began to move. But they were too late. The barrel plane taxied out of the cargo room and took to the air.

"What now?" asked Funky Kong. "Back home?"

"No," said Donkey Kong. "Make one more pass over the factory. With the automatic defense system down, we should be safe. I want to drop

all my remaining TNT barrels onto the factory. It may not be enough to take out the whole thing, but at least it will set them back a bit in their construction schedule."

As Funky swung the plane around, a strange sight appeared in the sky. The Kremling's army of evil flying pigs was taking to the air. The pink pigs flapped their gray wings and headed right for the barrel plane.

"What do we do now?" asked Diddy.

"I've got an idea," replied Funky as the pigs drew closer. "I didn't have the time or the help to do this the first time I met those flying swine.

"Donkey, Diddy, get to the back of the plane. Pull out the big barrels. Banana shakes are my favorite snack. I always keep a few barrels of the stuff on board in case I get hungry."

"What in monkey madness are you planning to do?" cried Cranky Kong. "Have a picnic with these pigs?"

"Nope," replied Funky. "I'm going to shake them up. Or I should say, shake them down!"

Funky pulled the plane higher into the sky.

When he was directly over the pigs, he opened one of the plane's doors. Donkey Kong and Diddy poured gallons and gallons of banana shakes out the doors.

The thick, sticky liquid covered the pigs' wings. One by one they lost control of their ability to fly, and each pig was forced to glide down to the ground.

"Nicely done, dudes," said Funky. "Now let's hit this joint and motor on out of here." Funky swung the plane around for a final TNT barrel-bombing run.

Suddenly something huge and terrifying rose from behind the factory. It was a zeppelin, a flying airship filled with lighter-than-air gas. This was the command ship of King K. Rool. The cruel image of Rool was painted on the zeppelin's side.

The massive airship fired deadly rockets at the tiny barrel plane. Only Funky's incredible skill as a pilot enabled him to dodge the speeding rockets, which detonated all around them.

"Take the plane up, Funky," said Donkey Kong. "I have an idea."

Funky flew straight up and over the zeppelin. Donkey Kong stood up. The wind blew back his fur. "You with me on this one, little buddy?" he asked Diddy.

Diddy Kong was nervous. The sight of the giant zeppelin frightened him, but he was sticking with his friend all the way. He stood up next to Donkey Kong. "I'm with you," he said. "Let's go!"

When Funky pulled directly over the zeppelin, Donkey Kong and Diddy leaped from the plane onto the zeppelin's huge bag.

"Hold on, Diddy!" shouted Donkey Kong. "Grab the bag tightly and follow me!" Donkey Kong led the way, climbing down the side of the giant bag, followed closely by Diddy. Even for the Kongs this was a very difficult climb.

When they reached the cabin, Donkey Kong kicked open the door and the Kongs slipped inside. Funky circled overhead, out of the view of the Kremlings and their rockets.

Once inside, Donkey Kong and Diddy swung into action. They took out the Kremling guards with double jumps, cartwheel attacks, and barrels left and right. As they ran through the airship they planted time-delayed TNT barrels everywhere. At the far end of the cabin, Donkey Kong kicked open a locked door and came face to face with King K. Rool.

"This ship is going down in a matter of minutes, Rool," said Donkey Kong.

"That's a shame, Kong," replied the Kremling leader. "But I won't be aboard when that happens!" The powerful Kremling pushed past Donkey Kong and Diddy and ran from the room.

"Let the coward go," said Donkey Kong. "He's just a big windbag, like his ship!" Donkey Kong pulled out the walkie-talkie. "All set, Funky," he said into the transmitter. "See you below!"

Donkey Kong and Diddy ran back to the door and leaped from the zeppelin. Funky flew by below and the two apes landed in the plane, right on top of Cranky.

"Why don't you watch where you're falling?" yelled Cranky.

"Sorry about that, Pops," apologized

Donkey Kong. "Okay, Funky, let's fly. That thing's going to blow any second."

Funky Kong turned back toward home. The Kongs saw King K. Rool's escape pod blast off from the zeppelin just as the TNT barrels exploded and the entire airship burst into flames.

"Look where it's going down!" shouted Diddy, pointing out the window.

The fiery zeppelin plunged through the air, landing right on top of the Kremlings' factory. The factory went up in a powerful explosion, putting an end to the Kremlings' evil plans.

"We got them!" cried Diddy.

"You were great, little buddy," replied Donkey Kong.

"Hey, I just realized something," said Funky. "I've got to get you dudes home in a hurry."

"What's the rush?" asked Donkey Kong.

"I've still got a passenger waiting for me on the other side of the island!" exclaimed Funky.

The Kongs all laughed as Funky Kong increased his speed and headed for their jungle home.